"Reviews"

"*Cocktails and Kicktails* brings back great memories for me. Its anarchic humour, funny stories and witty rhymes, plus some great recipes, conjure up the wild partying of the 1930's when I wrote my book. Bravo!" – *(Imagined Ghost of) Harry Craddock, famed bartender, author of the definitive cocktailer's bible The Savoy Cocktail Book and inventor of hundreds of drinks, including the Corpse Reviver No. 2*

"To introduce 'hypergolic' into a cocktail recipe and then to squeeze it into a rhyme as well is the work of genius. I've nominated the author for a Nobel prize." – *Just Buzzing, rocket entrepreneur*

"The study of Italian politics is a serious subject, particularly when it comes to Sr. Berlusconi. The ridiculous Scottie man that wrote this book with its silly stories and even sillier rhymes should *vaffanculo* back to the mountains in his tartan skirt." – *Martin I MarasChinoTrouser, Professor of Political History, The (left-leaning) University of Pisa*
   (PS "Hey, barista, what was I drinking? Il Cavalieri? Delishush, give me another pleash, hic. Cin Cin!)

"Can't understand what all the fuss is about cocktails. What's wrong with gin and water? Been living off it for almost a century." – *Vice Admiral Sir Hurley Rumtotter-Bigshot (retired) DSC (VHF)*

Cocktails
Kicktails

Cocktails & Kicktails

Life-saving Recipes and Rhymes to Lift Body and Soul

ROWAN BOOKS
EDINBURGH AND LONDON
2021

First published in Great Britain in 2021 by
Rowan Books, Edinburgh and London
www.rowanbooks.co.uk

ISBN-13: 978-1-7399877-0-1

Book design by Gareth Southwell,
art.garethsouthwell.com

Printed by Biddles Books, King's Lynn, Norfolk PE32 1SF

Contents

About the Author

Hugh Stewart grew up in the Grampian Mountains of Scotland, in a remote cottage without electricity. It lies just 50 feet below the house that until recently was the highest in the country.

Just 20 miles away as the grouse flies, lies Dufftown which has almost as many distilleries as houses. Here, the sought-after Balvenie whisky is made from water that flows over the bones of Stewart ancestors. As a boy Hugh loved the stories of people building illicit whisky stills in the glens; making his own whisky remains an ambition.

His first school was Corgarff Primary School. A lad who sat at the front called MacGregor was always first to put his hand up for the tattie pan so he could have the scrapings of mashed potato. This was excellent training for when the Minister came to talk about the dangers we might face. "What would you do if a stranger offered you strong drink?" the Minister asked. Quick as a flash, MacGregor's arm shot up. "Ask him to add water!" came the reply.

When Hugh was about ten he and a lifelong friend Charlie were invited to a children's highland reel party, with tea beforehand with Hugh's grandparents. Charlie had an upset tummy, threatening the party plan. Hugh's grandfather said "Follow me!" with that air of command that befits the full Admiral that he was. They reappeared from the pantry, Charlie with a wine glass full of browny-reddy liquid (port and brandy half and half). "Straight down!" came the command. Charlie obeyed, the tummy ache vanished and he spent the rest of the evening reeling in every possible sense.

These early influences led Hugh down the treacherous path of experimentation, the results of which are described in this book.

By profession, Hugh is a wannabe writer and striving sailor. By hobby, and to finance his professions, he is a venture capitalist, an occupation described as someone who pours petrol on to a blazing fire. Bit like mixing cocktails.

Preface

"Let's try the Elizabethan", said my American business partner David. He was a Texan, albeit an atypical one. He would come to the UK for a week every six months or so, during which he and I would test out the restaurants in Winchester. Nowadays, every chef with a reputation has a restaurant in Winchester, but in those days there were the Chinese, the Indian, the burger joint, the posh Hotel du Vin and... the Elizabethan. We'd flirted with going in on many an occasion but good sense had kept us out. Finally, we took the plunge.

It brought to mind the description of the library in Meryvn Peake's *Gormenghast* with Sawdust, the ageless librarian. The building had not changed since the days of Queen Bess. It was dark, dim and dusty and the food turned out to follow the same pattern. Even if the restaurant wasn't genuinely Elizabethan, the chicken certainly was.

David and I also experimented with drinks. At least I did, but he always stuck to his favourite, a *Martini*. One day I came across the poem by American writer Ogden Nash "A drink with something in it" and sent it to David with gusto (he replied by sending me "Under the Scotsman's Kilt", a marvellous song by Jim Stafford).

I loved the poem and would recite it whenever I had a *Martini* to hand. So, in part this book is a tribute to (Frederic) Ogden Nash. He was well known for his light verse and wrote over 500 poems, often with unconventional rhymes and made-up words, like "sellyfish" to rhyme with "jellyfish".

"A drink with something in it" became one of his best-known poems. Here is the magic:

> *There is something about a Martini,*
> *A tingle remarkably pleasant;*
> *A yellow, a mellow Martini;*
> *I wish I had one at present.*
>
> *There is something about a Martini,*
> *Ere the dining and dancing begin,*
> *And to tell you the truth,*
> *It is not the vermouth —*
> *I think that perhaps it's the gin.*

The rhyming pattern is: ABAB ACDDC which, after a few cocktails, sounds like Moby Dick's skipper meets Australian rock band.

The full version of "A drink with something in it" is included at the end of this book. It contains magical medically suicidal descriptions like:

> *There is something about an old-fashioned*
> *That kindles a cardiac glow*

This is a book of cocktails. Many are original, some are original variations on standards, and some are regular favourites. All have names that have amused me as I've thought them up. I hope they amuse you. Each one has a recipe and a poem in the ABAB ACDDC style.

But why life-saving cocktails? Well, one can imagine many situations where a cocktail could be a life-saver. Here's a couple:

- You're up before a firing squad (NB this could well happen: see the entry for *Il Cavaliere*). Your last request? A cocktail, of course, preferably one with lots of alcohol like the *Pampered Goose*. You don't want to hog it all so you share it with your executors (emphasis is important here, lest they think you want to write a will). Having concocted devilish drinks for decades you have a head like concrete, but they are not used to cocktails, particularly yours. You have earned valuable thinking time as your executors struggle in a discombobulated state.

- You're in a life raft in the North Atlantic after your ship has struck an iceberg. Morale is low, to the point where some of your shipmates are talking about throwing people off because there's not enough water (nonsense of course - you're surrounded by it). It's time for a big morale-booster to be followed by an uplifting singsong – think "Land of Hope and Glory". Try something with fizz in it – maybe a *Berlusconi* or a *Lagonda*.

Though useful, these situations are not the reason for the book's title. That answer lies with legendary actress Mae West, one of whose famous lines was allegedly: "This kicktail's got a cock like a mule". So, in our family, cocktails have always been known as kicktails. Still not there with the life-saving? Apart from some great one-liners Mae West also gave her name, thanks to her gorgeous figure, to the voluptuous life-jackets of old, here modelled by King George VI and Queen Elizabeth.

Quite a few of the cocktails in this book are named after Italians. This is mainly because a lot of cocktail ingredients are Italian – think Campari, Martini and maraschino for starters. But also because Italy is rich with colourful figures, 'Bunga Bunga' Berlusconi being one, who generate outrageous stories that one can write about and characterise in liquor and rhyme.

I hope you enjoy this book and trying these drinks. The book refers to them as cocktails but you may slip into Mae West's lingo after the first couple.

Hugh Stewart

Know Your Limits

This book contains recipes for twenty-three cocktails, all but two of which are alcoholic (by the way, the non-alcoholic ones are both delicious). They often contain more than one alcohol. So please enjoy these cocktails but don't let alcohol become your master. Stay within your limits and within prescribed guidelines, be aware of the risks and if you're worried that you're becoming dependent, seek advice.

The UK Chief Medical Officers recommend that adults do not regularly drink more than 14 units of alcohol a week.

A single pub measure of spirit = 1 unit

Drink Responsibly

www.drinkaware.co.uk

A sparkle full of life's zest   The Flora Dora

the
Cocktails

Cocktails at a Glance

Cocktail	Liqueurs	Spirit
Asian Flew	maraschino	gin
L'Avvocato	advocaat, Strega	
Barbie Doll		light rum
Berlin Berlusconi	Campari	vodka
Breachacha Prayer	Cointreau	gin
Bum's Rush	Aperol	light rum
A Frisky Malt		whisky
Gin Jams	Campari	gin
Henry's Flora Dora	Cointreau, crème de framboise	gin
Highland Bull	sherry	whisky
Il Cavalieri	maraschino	gin
Lagonda		bourbon
Leith Pre-Mix	Cointreau, crème de framboise	light rum
Lovely Rita	Triple Sec or Cointreau	tequila
(Non) Prosecuto	Campari	
Noonday Gun		
The Ogden Nash	dry vermouth e.g. Martini	gin
Pampered Goose	Cointreau, crème de fraise	gin
Peacock Flamingo		gin
Proud Mary	sherry	vodka
Red Snapper	madeira	gin
Ryders on the Storm		gin
Shopaholic	Campari, Cointreau, dry vermouth	gin

Fizz	Juice	Extras	Garnish
	lemon	honey water	basil, cherry, lemon
Champagne	lime		lime
	lime, rhubarb	soda water	lime
	orange		orange
	lime	Fentiman's Pink Ginger	seaweed, (sand!)
	lime	ginger beer	lime, mint
		water	nae garnish
	lime	tonic	lime
	lime, raspberry	ginger beer	lime, mint, raspberry
	lemon	consommé/ bouillon, spicy bits	heather, moss etc
prosecco	blood orange		cherry, orange
Champagne	lemon	honey water, bitters	lemon
clementine	clementine, lime, raspberry	ginger beer	lime, raspberry
	lime		lime
prosecco	blood orange		orange
	lime	ginger beer, soda water	lime, mint
			lemon or olive
prosecco	grapefruit		grapefruit
		blue pea flowers, tonic	lemon
	lemon, tomato	spicy bits	celery, lemon
lemon	lemon, tomato	spicy bits	celery, lemon
apple cider	lime	ginger beer	apple, lime, mint
			olive

4

Asian Flew

I walked into Gerry's, the holy grail for cocktail fixers in London's Soho and asked for a bottle of maraschino. "Aha, you're making an *Aviation*." "Sort of" I replied, "it's an *Aviation* with a difference."

An *Aviation* combines gin, lemon juice and maraschino, and optionally crème de violette. Maraschino is an Italian liqueur made from cherries but it's not a schnapps like Kirsch, it's oozy, viscous and slightly sweet. Think Cointreau but with cherries. I was once served a delicious cocktail in the Hong-Kong owned Mandarin Hotel in Knightsbridge and asked what was in it – the answer is what I have christened *Asian Flew*. It's an *Aviation* with a dash of honey and fresh basil and a touch of the Orient.

These verses were written in New Zealand, hence the reference to possum merino, an über-warm combo of possum fur and merino wool and to the tui, a sort of giant pigeon that gets drunk by eating alcoholic berries in Kauri trees. Sometimes they overdo it and fall off. Kauris grow to 40-50 metres. Ouch!

Purists will argue New Zealand is not geographically in Asia but what the hell! What's a few thousand miles matter when you've got a bellyful of boozy berries?

Asian Flew

There is something about Asian Flew
A lift off that's rapid but sweet
You soar high on the wind like a tui
Life's better at ten thousand feet

There is something about Asian Flew
A warmth like a possum merino
Then out of the blue
Comes a boom like Mach 2
The thrust as gin meets maraschino.

Ingredients

- 4 parts gin
- 1 part maraschino
- 1 part lemon juice
- 1/2 part honey water
- Fresh basil
- Cocktail glasses

A tui contemplates his future

Method

1. Mix the gin, maraschino and lemon juice
2. Add a few drops of honey water
3. Chill in the cocktail shaker
4. Pour and garnish with maraschino cherries, a lemon twist and basil leaves, roughly torn if large
5. Repeat as necessary, but not in trees

L'Avvocato

You really can't have a cocktail that uses advocaat without calling it _L'Avvocato_, can you? The head of Fiat, Gianni Agnelli, was known as _L'Avvocato_ (the 'Lawyer'), due to his original training. He built Fiat into an industrial powerhouse when, in 1966, he took over running the company founded by his grandfather.

Apart from producing some fun cars (I had a 124 Sport, a super machine with two gloriously sounding twin-choke Weber carburettors, good looks and Wolfrace wheels), Fiat was also famed for its test track on the roof of its Lingotto factory in Turin, immortalised in _The Italian Job_.

Agnelli was known for many things, including his love of beautiful art and beautiful women. It was a fight over the latter that caused him to be shot in a bar by a German officer during the Second World War (Italy was on the German side). Fortunately, unlike the subject of Robert Service's wonderful poem "The Shooting of Dan McGrew" (about a girl called Lou), Agnelli survived and went on to marry a princess.

The cocktail has Champagne for style (or use prosecco), lime juice to balance the advocaat's sweetness and Strega to give it an Italian twist. It's a variation on a _Valanga_, the Italian word for snowball.

Vroom Vroom! Cin Cin!

L'Avvocato

There is something about L'Avvocato
A twin-choked concoction of joy
Throw it back with a shot of bravado
You're now an Italian playboy

There is something about L'Avvocato
The eggnog is viscous and yellow
Strega's the witch
Your brain to enrich
Add fizz as a natural bedfellow.

Fiat's Lingotto Test Track

Ingredients

- 4 parts advocaat
- 1 part lime juice
- 1 part Strega
- 4 parts Champagne or prosecco
- Slice of lime
- Champagne glasses

Method

1. Mix the advocaat, lime juice and Strega in a cocktail shaker and chill
2. Pour into glasses
3. Top up with fizz, adding slowly as it will bubble up
4. Stir gently
5. Garnish with lime
6. Repeat with second choke as necessary

Fiat 124 Sport Coupé

Barbie Doll

Spring brings joy for many reasons – Paris, rhododendrons, the bird is on the wing (no you fool – the wing is on the bird!). Plus of course, delicious pink, tart rhubarb. How could one let all that rhubarb appear in the shops without making a cocktail from it? Cracking taste, cracking colour. And interestingly rhubarb is actually a vegetable unlike a tomato which is a fruit. Very modish too, as it was imported to Europe from China along the Silk Road via Istanbul. Chinese rhubarb is also said to be the answer to a heavy night - see the section on Hangover Cures – so maybe they had humdingers back in those days. Perhaps you can pre-load a cure by having a rhubarb cocktail?

The main thing about rhubarb is tartness. It tastes tart, it goes well in a tart. Quite simply, it is tarty.

Now for the cocktail. Where do we start? With the letter R for rhubarb? You need to keep things simple when making cocktails – mental functions can get impaired. Bit like George Foreman naming all his sons George: "If you're going to get hit as many times as I've been hit by Mohammad Ali, Joe Frazier, Ken Norton, Evander Holyfield, you're not going to remember many names."

So that means RRRum. It needs to be light (aka white) rum to catch that clean, zingy style.

9

Barbie Doll

There is something about Barbie Doll
A body that's playful and varied
A look that's decidedly AWOL
As tartness and liquor are married

There is something about Barbie Doll
The rhubarb's so vibrant and juicy
The rum starts the show
Add a dash of Cointreau.
And your doll acts all moll and seducey.

Ingredients

- 4 parts light rum
- ½ part Cointreau maximum – really just a dash otherwise it will take charge
- 1 part lime juice
- 4 parts rhubarb syrup.
- (optional) top up with soda water
- Cocktail glasses

Method

Barbie Doll

1. Spoon crushed ice into stylish thin glasses
2. Add the rum, Cointreau and lime juice
3. Fold in the rhubarb syrup
4. Top up with soda water if the syrup makes it a bit too viscous
5. Garnish with lime slice
6. Repeat playfully

Berlin Berlusconi

Back in the 1970's, at the time of the Winter of Discontent, I lived in a stunningly ugly block of flats in Pimlico which a friend had christened East Berlin. Visitors had to be anaesthetised. This cocktail is one of the attempts. It's basically a *Screwdriver* with an Italian twist, being the addition of Campari. The bitterness of the Campari fights with the sweetness of the orange juice while the vodka gives it drive. Decades later as Silvio Berlusconi came to power, the as yet unnamed cocktail came to be called a *Berlin Berlusconi*. Why Berlusconi? International statesman with an Italian twist? Despite the fact that Italians knew the ex-cruise line crooner turned media tycoon was a bit of a rogue, they kept on voting for him because as the editor of La Stampa once said he had "the ear", he knew how to make Italians laugh. As a result of combining bitterness with this touch of sweetness he was Italian Prime Minister for nine years, making him the longest-serving post-war Prime Minister. He was also popular internationally, holding the record for hosting the highest number of G8 Summits (three). And of course, he was famous for "bunga bunga" parties...

Berlin Berlusconi

There is something about Berlusconi
The roguish appeal that swings voters
Is the hair really his or just phoney?
Who cares, he's got plenty of doters

There is something about Berlusconi
'Ere the crooning and swooning begin
A dash of Campari
Like zest of Ferrari
This is the new Cardinal Sin.

Ingredients

- 5 parts vodka
- 2 parts Campari
- 7 parts orange juice
- Large goblets or tumblers

East Berlin Cold War era apartments

Silvio Berlusconi

Method

1. Put a couple of large ice cubes into each glass
2. Add the vodka and Campari
3. Top up with same amount of orange juice
4. Garnish with a slice of orange
5. Ripetere se necessario

The Breachacha Prayer

My wife and I were sailing in company with friends on a meander around the West Coast of Scotland and had anchored in Loch Breachacha on the island of Coll. This is an atmospheric place complete with not one but two castles (the more modern one being the "Newcastle" of the north). "Cocktails on the beach at 18.00" came the signal. Tim and Sophie produced a *Dark 'n' Stormy* (dark rum and ginger beer). I rummaged around in the booze locker and put together what Sophie named *The Breachacha Prayer* because it reminded her of the *Maiden's Prayer* (gin, Cointreau, Triple Sec, orange juice and lemon juice) that her father-in-law used to make. We were well fuelled. A blazing bonfire surrounded by empty chairs added a surreal feel, and the opening for a caption competition, the winner being "Red Hot Chilli Piper". Uplifted by the music of piper Henry, the evening morphed into a ceilidh culminating in dancing "Strip the Willow" in seaboots on soft sand. This proved to be quite a cardiovascular workout, or perhaps what Ogden Nash called a "cardiac glow". Thankfully all survived.

If you want to get a party going, wherever you may be, pray for a *Breachacha* – and maybe a *Dark 'n' Stormy* too.

The Breachacha Prayer

There is something about Breachacha
Meanderers piped in with the tide
A dancing, entrancing Breachacha
Stripping willow in sand by lochside

There is something about Breachacha
A beachful of fire-funnelled fun
Gin, Cointreau and lime
Make a craiching good time
Add Fentiman's Ginger – job done!

Ingredients

Red Hot Chilli Piper

- 4 parts gin, seawater-chilled
- 1 part Cointreau
- 1 part lime juice
- Less than a part of Fentiman's Pink Ginger
- Plastic picnic glasses

Method

Strip the Willow

1. Chill the gin, Cointreau and lime juice in the sea (or in a shaker if you haven't an ocean handy)
2. Top up with just enough Pink Ginger to turn the drink pink
3. Garnish with seaweed and the odd grain of sand if you like a grittier cocktail
4. Repeat as many times as your cardiac system can take

The Bum's Rush

Okay, it's truth time. Hands up those who have not been given the Bum's Rush from some dodgy dive? Nobody?! At least you're honest (oh yeah?!). Most definitions of a Bum's Rush talk of a swift and forcible ejection. The Merriam-Webster dictionary says the first known use of the term was in 1910 although people were evicted for sinning a lot earlier than that – what about Adam and Eve (Genesis 3: 22-24)?

The name is derived from a magi-blend of ingredients and themes, but have too many of these and you may be joining the evicted. Choose light rum, as it allows the Aperol to drive the colour, but if you haven't got any to hand, dinna fache as we Scots say. A dark rum will work and once you've had a couple you'll be colour blind anyway. If you haven't any Aperol, use Campari, but it's a bit stronger both in taste and alcohol so just a half measure.

The Bum's Rush

There is something about a Bum's Rush
The drama of instant eviction
Heads down for a bitterbite crush
And the hope of avoiding conviction

There is something about a Bum's Rush
A fusion of bitter and sweet
An oomph from the rum
Will make your heart strum
And sweep your top half from your feet.

Ingredients

- 4 parts light rum
- 1 part Aperol
- 4 parts ginger beer
- 1 part lime juice
- Mint leaves
- Large goblets or tumblers

A FINE ESTAB

Method

1. Put a couple of large ice cubes into each glass
2. Add the rum, Aperol and lime juice
3. Top up with ginger beer
4. Garnish with fresh lime and a sprig of mint
5. Repeat as necessary until evicted (or just before)

A Frisky Malt

Whisky, or uisge-beatha in the Gaelic. Uisge means water and uisge-beatha is the water of life. Like eau de vie in France. Your dram may be accompanied by a drop of water or not, as you like. Then you can raise your glass with a "sláinte mhaith!" (pronounced "slanj-a-va", often abbreviated to "slanj") meaning good health. Or you go for a more fatal sort of toast like:

> *Here's tae us*
> *Wha's like us?*
> *Damn few*
> *And they're a' deid*

However you toast it, whisky will put life in your party – unless they're a' deid. Live life to the full, especially on a boat.

A Frisky Malt

There is something about a malt whisky
A drink one can sink without guilt
A risky, a frisky malt whisky
Makes you want to cavort in your kilt

There is something about a malt whisky
'Ere the burrling and whirrling begin
No time to discuss
Just cry "Here's tae us!"
And mind that ye nae bash your shin.

The Author and his Wife...   *... dance a Foredeck Reel*

 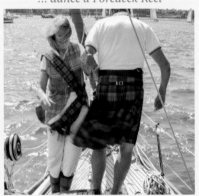

Ingredients

- 4 parts malt whisky
- 1 dash water (optional)
- 1 part hope

Method

1. Pour the whisky
2. "Nose" it
3. Taste a wee bit
4. Add a tiny dash of water (or not)
5. Nae garnish
6. Repeat pour/nose/ taste as necessary

18

Gin Jams

*G*in Jams is a gin and tonic, but with a difference! Friends Ash and Christine introduced me to a drink called a *Hartley* that they'd found in a cocktail book. It was a G&T with a dash of Campari and orange juice. Good but not as good as *Gin Jams* which takes things one bold step further by using lime juice. This gives delicate balance to the sweetness from the tonic and Campari. Why *Gin Jams*? The older reader will recall a brand of jam called Hartley's New Jam, introduced in 1963. *Gin Jams* is the obvious sequitur.

Ironically, Hartley's New Jam was introduced by Schweppes who bought Hartley's in 1959, so this is not the first time tonic and jam have been (con)fused.

With its nod to pyjamas the name conjures up the hedonistic life style of 1960's Chelsea. Think Afghan hounds (and/or coats), miniskirts, the Stones, Twiggy and lots of partying.

Gin Jams

There is something about a Gin Jams
A sexy new twist on a favourite
Try it late as you don your jim-jams
Or sip early and slowly to savour it

There is something about a Gin Jams
Adds panache to mere gin and tonic
With lime's tarty twist
And Campari's lift
The fusion becomes polyphonic.

Ingredients

- 4 parts gin
- 3 parts tonic
- 1 part lime juice
- A dash of Campari
- Large goblets or tumblers

Hartley's New Jam

Pyjama Party anyone?

Method

1. Put a couple of big ice cubes in each glass
2. Add the gin, tonic and lime juice
3. Add a dash of Campari, just enough to turn the drink pink
4. Garnish with a slice of lime
5. Repeat as necessary till it's time for bed

Henry's FloraDora

My claim to originality here is that Flora is my younger daughter, often known as FloraDora, and Henry her lovely husband (who came up with the cocktail shaker idea for the App). We had this marvellous cocktail at their wedding. It's loosely modelled on *Hendrick's FloraDora* but with added goodies to give it even more zest.

At its heart is the combo of gin, fortified with a dash of Cointreau, and raspberries, with their sweetness balanced with lime. I've also chucked in some crème de framboise to add bodily viscosity. The ginger beer rounds it off and makes it eminently quaffable.

It's worth taking the time to make your own raspberry syrup. The bought stuff is hideously sweet and will dominate the drink. Make a decent sized batch and freeze what you don't need.

To the bride and groom!

Henry's FloraDora

There is something about FloraDora
A marriage of everything best
A happily romantic aura
And a sparkle full of life's zest

There is something about FloraDora
The pinkness of Scottish raspberry
A dash of Cointreau
Will make your heart glow
As your guests get increasingly merry.

Ingredients

- 4 parts gin
- 1 part crème de framboise
- Less than 1 part Cointreau
- 1 part raspberry syrup
- 2 parts lime juice
- 6 parts ginger beer
- Large goblets or tumblers

Henry and FloraDora

Method

1. Put a couple of big ice cubes in each glass
2. Add the gin, framboise, Cointreau, lime and raspberry syrup
3. Top up with equal amount of ginger beer
4. Garnish with a slice of lime, some raspberries and a sprig of mint
5. Once in a lifetime

The Highland Bull

It's a miserably cold winter's day. You've been trying to film shearwaters on the island of Rum (optimistic given it's winter). You are shivering. The last thing you want is a fancy fruit-based cocktail with lots of ice. Fear not! The answer is a *Highland Bull*. This is a Scots take on a *Bullshot*. If you've never had it, it's a cross between a thin soup and a *Proud Mary*. Its heart is beef consommé though you could make a vegan version using a vegetable bouillon. The Scots variation is to use whisky instead of vodka. I feel it is almost sacrilegious to add anything to whisky other than a drop of water so I say this with some reservation, but try it. It sounds vile but is actually delicious. However, don't waste a fancy malt, just use cooking whisky.

The Highland Bull

There is something about Highland Bull
It's beefy and horny and muscly
Feel the warmth warp through your skull
You'll soon charge a lot more robustly

There is something about Highland Bull
A fortified soup from the glens
A day spent al fresco
Fired up by Tabasco
Will gie a' your system a cleanse.

Horny Highland Bull
with heather and moss

Ingredients

- 3 parts whisky
- ½ part sherry
- 1 part lemon juice
- 6 parts beef consommé
- Worcestershire sauce
- Tabasco
- Celery salt
- Pepper
- Horn mugs

Method

1. Mix all ingredients
2. Microwave for a minute or two (depends on batch size)
3. Put in a Thermos flask
4. Take up a mountain in mid-winter
5. Garnish with heather, moss etc to taste
6. Repeat as necessary till you're charged (*police or bull – Ed?*)

Il Cavaliere

This is my second Berlusconi cocktail. He was nicknamed 'Il Cavaliere' (The Knight) after he was awarded the Order of Merit for Labour (though he later resigned following his conviction for tax fraud). So why name a cocktail *Il Cavaliere*? The simple answer is that the ingredients are all Italian apart from the gin, the name's got swing and there's a bit of a story.

Emperor Maximilian I of Mexico was commander-in-chief of the Austrian navy. Map observers today would think that a joke because Austria is landlocked. But, back in the mid-19th century the Austrian Empire was formed from the ashes of the dissolved Holy Roman Empire, (incidentally described by Voltaire as being none of these things) and contained ports like Trieste. Maximilian did a fine job of building up the navy, as a result of which he got to have Mexico and became its first (Austrian) Emperor. Things went pear-shaped after a couple of years and Maximilian wound up in front of a firing squad. In those days a "shot" meant more than a dose of firewater. The connection between *Il Cavaliere* and Maximilian is tenuous but involves Sicily. It was, after all, part of the Holy Roman Empire after the Treaty of Utrecht (1713). And it rhymes.

If you do find yourself in front of a firing squad call for a cocktail as your last request and share it with your executors. Escape amidst their discombobulation.

Il Cavaliere

There is something about Cavaliere
A knight you are sure to remember
A balance of flavours so cheery
You'll park the tax bill till December

There is something about Cavaliere
The cherries, the fizz, the Sicilian
But mind the drink's power
As a fourth you devour
Or you'll wind up like old Maximilian.

Ingredients

- 1 part gin
- 1 part maraschino
- 2 parts prosecco
- 4 parts orange juice, preferably from Sicilian blood oranges (so there is a point to Waitrose, after all)
- Large goblets or tumblers

Method

1. Put a couple of big ice cubes into each glass
2. Add the gin, maraschino and orange juice
3. Add the prosecco
4. Garnish with a slice of orange and maraschino cherries
5. Repeat as necessary, or until shot

26

Lagonda

You may think this cocktail is named after the Aston Martin Lagonda car, particularly those that know I am lucky enough to drive a beautiful DB7 Vantage Volante that was a present from my wonderful wife Wendy. If the brand copyright police raid us we will naturally deny the derivation.

Instead, the name stems from the gorgeous Lagonda gorge in Ohio, after which the car firm was named by its founder Wilbur Gunn, an opera singer turned engineer, who was born there but moved to Britain. He had the distinction of winning the Moscow-St Petersburg trial in 1910 leading to a surge in Russian sales prior to WWI. Perhaps pre-1917 Russia was an appropriate market for a car of revolutionary design?

This cocktail conjures up the flowing luxury of the Lagonda, combining Bourbon royalty with Champagne's panache. You question the royalty? No! Bourbon was the name of the French royal family prior to the 1789 revolution. The application of the name to whiskey is thought to stem from Bourbon Street in New Orleans. No doubt you will pick up the Champagne's biscuity (chocolate Bourbon?) notes. If not, let them eat cake!

The picture is of a Lagonda crossing a river, the gorgeous gorge perhaps? "Lagonda Fords Lagonda" (though it smacks of impure automotive heritage) or "Lagonda in Lagonda?"

Whichever, recline in the leather upholstery and enjoy! Perhaps wear a Mae West.

Lagonda

There is something about a Lagonda
She's lively, she's long and she's louche
A sinuous, sleek anaconda
A liquified gold amuse-bouche

There is something about a Lagonda
You'd hardly call Champagne suburban
While dashed Angostura
Befits a grand tourer
Whose roots like the royals lie in Bourbon.

Ingredients

- 4 parts bourbon
- 1½ parts honey water
- 1 part lemon juice
- 3 dashes of Angostura bitters
- 3 parts Champagne
- Large goblets or tumblers

Lagonda in ford

Method

1. Mix the bourbon, honey and lemon juice and cool in a cocktail shaker
2. Pour into glasses
3. Top up with chilled Champagne
4. Garnish with lemon twist
5. Repeat as necessary (unless you're at the wheel of your Aston)

28

Leith Pre-Mix

My wife and I had been walking at Cramond, to the north of Edinburgh, with friends Michael and Annemarie. On our return, we passed a cement works with a sign "Leith Pre-Mix". What a great name for a cocktail!

Michael and I talked ingredients as we drove, then dived into the kitchen to experiment. Leith is the port of Edinburgh, famed in the tongue-twister "The Leith police dismisseth us". It used to be seedy, as befits a major port, with many a discombobulated sailor sat on a bollard gazing at the (often scantily-dressed) wildlife. All that has changed: Leith is now crammed with smart restaurants and yuppy flats with water frontage.

We imagined a ship from the Caribbean loaded with rum, limes, clementines and ginger. Maybe a French ship (the *Auld Alliance*) so they'd have Cointreau to tune with the clementines. We'd then add the vital Scottish component: raspberries from the "The Berryfields O Blair" (nothing to do with the ex-PM, this is Blairgowrie, home of the Scottish raspberry), made famous in Belle Stewart's song of that name, whose verses include:

There's corner-boys fae Glesgae,
Kettle-boilers fae Lochee,
There's miners fae the pits o Fife,
Mill-workers fae Dundee

And fisherfolk fae Peterheid
And tramps fae everywhere
Aa looking fir a livin aff
The berry fields o blair

Leith Pre-Mix

There is something about a Leith Pre-Mix
Its seafaring scent is so seedy
It will hit your sang-froid for a six
So beware if you tend to be greedy

There is something about a Leith Pre-Mix
As the contents begin to ferment
Your heart will soon strum
To the pace of the rum
And your stomach will turn to cement.

Ingredients

- 4 parts dark rum
- 1 part Cointreau
- Less than 1 part crème de framboise
- 1 part lime juice
- Less than 1 part clementine juice
- 1 part raspberry syrup
- 7ish parts ginger beer
- Large goblets or tumblers

Method

1. Put a couple of big ice cubes into each glass
2. Add everything except the ginger beer
3. Top up with equal amount of ginger beer
4. Garnish with slices of lime and clementine and with fresh raspberries
5. Repeat as necessary, but beware the Leith police.

Try saying "The Leith police dismisseth us" after your third!

The 'Porters Stone' from a 17th Century wine-merchant's house in Leith

Lovely Rita

No pretence here. This is a *Margarita* with a fancy name. The *Margarita* is one of the world's great cocktails so I wouldn't dare try to improve it.

Can you imagine a traffic warden (or Civil Enforcement Officer as they are now) with a *Lovely Rita* in her hand? That would certainly enforce some civil behaviour!

There are many different stories about the invention of the *Margarita*: who, where, when, why. Most of them involve Mexico or Mexicans and in quite a few a beautiful girl called Margarita. That's good enough for me. Remember, if you go to Mexico, that "x" is pronounced "h" and follow Mae West's advice: "travel to Mehico in a tahicab".

One word on the glasses. Some people like the rims to be coated with salt; I don't and know others who don't, so do ask beforehand. For those that do, run a wedge of lime round the rim of the glass and then dip it into some salt. Or just salt half the rim.

Lovely Rita

There is something about Lovely Rita
She's Mehico's sehiest show
The drink that's as fast as a cheetah
It'll make you get up and go!

There is something about Lovely Rita
With her notes of mile high agave
While chilled Triple Sec
Will thrill an Aztec
And kick off a Mehican Wavee.

Ingredients

- 4 parts tequila
- 1½ parts Triple Sec
  (or Cointreau)
- 1 part lime juice
- Salt (subject to desire)
- Cocktail glasses

Margarita (actually Mae West)

Method

1. Chill the tequila, Triple
   Sec and lime juice in a
   cocktail shaker
2. Pour, having pre-salted
   the glasses if wanted
3. Garnish with slices of
   lime
4. Repita según sea
   necesario

(Non) Prosecuto

This my third, and final, Berlusconi cocktail. One of the many astonishing things about Berlusconi is that he has avoided being convicted for all alleged crimes other than tax fraud. According to many sources one of his techniques for avoiding successful prosecution was to get the law changed so being Prime Minister was almost a necessity.

AC Milan was owned by Berlusconi for 30 years till he sold it to a Chinese group. Opinion is divided about his reign: some loved the glitz and the success on the field, others regret the huge debts, relegations and later decline in performance. A bit like the Italian economy during Berlusconi's reign.

In September 2020 he got the COVID-19 virus and spent 11 days in hospital. Quite dangerous for someone aged 83. As he left hospital he said "Once again, I've got away with it!". You've got to admire the rogue.

The (non) Prosecuto is a blend of Campari, freshly-squeezed orange juice and prosecco. Deliciously refreshing. It's like a Mimosa except that it has Campari to add intrigue, a vital ingredient in any Italian cocktail. Do try to use blood oranges as the colour is gorgeous.

(Non) Prosecuto

There is something about Prosecuto
A delicate balance of thrills
Like AC Milan plays Subbuteo
With Houdini's escapist skills

There is something about Prosecuto
A refreshingly red burst of bliss
It's bitter and sweet
Like a Silvio tweet
And bubbles with Sicily's kiss.

Ingredients

- 3 parts Campari
- 2 parts orange juice – preferably from Sicilian blood oranges
- 6 parts prosecco
- Large goblets or tumblers

Method

1. Put a couple of big ice cubes into each glass
2. Add the Campari and orange juice
3. Top up with prosecco
4. Garnish with a slice of orange
5. Repeat as you judge necessary

Noonday Gun

Back to the Aston Martin DB7. We were staying with friends Avril and Vern in Somerset and went to a delightful pub for Sunday lunch. The other guys were all drinking pints but with 420 hp under my right foot I didn't want a drop of alcohol before the long drive home. That was after all what Niki Lauda and James Hunt battled with in their epic duels brought to life in the excellent film *Rush*. Therefore no booze for me, but I wanted to join the party by drinking a pint, so I ordered half a pint of lime and soda and half a pint of ginger beer with lots of ice in a pint glass. Delicious and cooling. A few weeks later I met our lawyer Andrew for lunch and ordered the same thing. He'd grown up in East Africa and said people used to drink that with a few dashes of bitters.

So I added the bitters. Then another friend Roger said "Oh yes, it's called a *Gunners*". I've tried ordering a *Gunners* in various bars but am faced with a blank look. So, I'm keeping the gun theme and as Roger spent part of his military career in Hong Kong, I'm naming it the *Noonday Gun* after the former naval gun at East Point in Causeway Bay, which is fired every day at noon.

The sort of refreshing non-alcoholic drink you need before deciphering complex maths or driving a powerful motor.

Noonday Gun

There is something about Noonday Gun
Refreshing and quite ceremonial
A trigger to have some fast fun
Or figure a tough polynomial

There is something about Noonday Gun
As lime zests with ginger and bitters
Just like a cold stream
It's a febrifuge dream
You'll be cool as befits all big hitters.

Ingredients

- ½ pint of lime and soda
- ½ pint of ginger beer
- 3 dashes of Angostura bitters
- Lime, mint and nasturtium flowers
- Pint glass

The Noonday Gun at Causeway Bay, Hong Kong

Method

1. Put a few big ice cubes into each glass
2. Add ingredients
3. Garnish with a slice of lime, a sprig of mint and perhaps some nasturtium flowers which are lovely and peppery
4. Repeat till you go bang

The Ogden Nash

aka Martini

Y ou might well ask what a book of innovative cocktails is doing
with a recipe for a *Martini*. The answer is that this book owes
its inspiration to Ogden Nash's poem "A Drink With Something
In It", the first verse of which is reproduced here. It would
therefore be rude not to include the *Martini*, and consequently,
his poem. And I'm naming the drink an *Ogden Nash* by way of
tribute.

There's much speculation about the ideal ratio: 20:1, 10:1 or
even 1:1 if you inhabit dives that don't know their cocktail arse
(tail? Geddit?) from their 'lift your' elbow. Some favour coating
the ice in vermouth in a shaker and then chucking away the
liquid. One of my favourite recommendations is Nöel Coward's,
being to 'wave the gin bottle in the general direction of Italy' – a
kind of quantum ratio.

The Ogden Nash

There is something about a Martini
A tingle remarkably pleasant
A yellow, a mellow Martini
I wish I had one at present

There is something about a Martini
'Ere the dining and dancing begin
And to tell you the truth
It's not the vermouth —
I think that perhaps it's the gin.

Ogden Nash

Ingredients

- Gin
- Dry vermouth, e.g. Martini – mix ratio à choix. Or you could be stylish and use Noilly Prat – a "gin and French"
- Ice
- Cocktail glasses

Method

1. Put a couple of ice cubes in a cocktail glass
2. Add the gin and vermouth
3. Stir gently to chill (unless you're Bond) then chuck the ice
4. Garnish with an olive or a lemon twist
5. Repeat with a line of verse between each

Pampered Goose

Pampered Goose was so named because it rhymed with the French word for grapefruit "Pamplemousse". It also rhymes with 'Spruce Goose', the name of Howard Hughes' vast eight-engined flying boat (more accurately slightly flying since it only flew once) that was the forerunner of the Hercules. Go to **www.aviationgeek.com** to learn more about the 'Spruce Goose' and for a link to a video of its flying with Hughes at the controls.

Grapefruit is a great cocktail ingredient because it has an edgy bite to it. Get red ones if you can – your *Pampered Goose* will be a gorgeous colour. The Cointreau and the crème de fraise (or framboise) counteract the edginess in a hedonistic dynamic tension aided and abetted by a good slug of prosecco. But don't give it to anyone taking statins: the combo of grapefruit and statins can lead to confusion and memory loss. Sounds like a standard cocktail effect!

This is a long cocktail – long-legged, long-necked even, like the Big Bopper's girl.

Pampered Goose

There is something about Pampered Goose
You'll float high in the sky in one hike
Long-necked like a goose you'll feel loose
"Oooh Baby, that is what I like"

There is something about Pampered Goose
A prosecco-propelled effervescence
Take ripe pamplemousse
Add Cointreau to spruce
The effect is unbridled quintessence.

Ingredients

- 6 parts gin
- 2 parts Cointreau
- 1 part crème de fraise
- 8 parts pamplemousse juice
- Many parts prosecco
- Large goblets or tumblers

Method

Howard Hughes' 'Spruce Goose'

1. Put a couple of big ice cubes into each glass
2. Add the gin, Cointreau, crème de fraise and pamplemousse
3. Top up with equal amount of prosecco
4. Garnish with slices of strawberry
5. Repeat as necessary (as long as you have altitude)

40

Peacock Flamingo

A friend Clive told me that in British Columbia he'd drunk some gin which was blue but turned pink when you added tonic. I was intrigued and did some homework.

The trick is Butterfly-Blue Pea Flowers (aka the curiously named Asian Pigeonwings) from the Clitoria(!) ternatea plant. They're used in Vietnam and Thailand for making tea and as a food dye. The clever bit is that they change colour from a peacock-blue to a flamingo-pink a little when you add lemon juice and a lot when you add tonic. You can buy the flowers online. 10g will keep you going for some time – no need to order a sackful!

Got the blues? Try a *Peacock Flamingo* and in moments you'll be in the pink!

Peacock Flamingo

There is something about a Flamingo
A peacockish strutting of style
A pinkness that makes one cry "Bingo!"
It is sure to be sipped with a smile

There is something about a Flamingo
As your glass fairly bubbles with tonic
The changing of hue
To bright pink from bright blue
Gives a sense that is truly hedonic.

Ingredients

- Gin
- Butterly-Blue Pea flowers
- Tonic
- Slice of lemon
- Large tumbler

A peacock morphs into a flamingo

Method

1. Mix a bottle at a time
2. Put half a dozen flowers in a plastic jug, cover with gin, microwave for 1 minute, add the rest of the gin bottle and chill
3. Then, for one cocktail:
   i. Put ice and lemon in a tumbler
   ii. Add a decent slug of Peacock Flamingo gin
   iii. Ask your guests to add tonic themselves and enjoy their delight!
4. Repeat as necessary (as long as you can stand on one leg)

Proud Mary

*P*roud Mary is a bit of a cheat. It's just a Mary, Virgin or Bloody. Having said that how could one say *just* a Mary. It is undeniably a classic drink with a hefty kick to start the morning/ day/night, even in Virgin mode. 'Proud Mary' was a hit for Creedence Clearwater Revival in 1971, a song about a river steamer. As you sink your drink think Mississippi, muddy creeks and gamblers.

My take on a *Mary*, of which I am duly proud, is ideally made the day before because that allows the garlic to seep through the pores of the tomato juice and make it unforgettable, both for you and no doubt for anyone nearby. As in the intro to 'Green Onions' in the original *American Graffiti*, "it helps to keep them vampires away".

While on the subject of tomatoes here's a philosophical joke: "What's red and invisible?" Answer: "No tomatoes".

You'll need the bloody version after that.

43

Proud Mary

There is something about a Proud Mary
A redness that's oozy and viscous
Be it virgin or bloody it's hairy
Your light head will spin like a discus

There is something about a Proud Mary
As rocket fuel impacts tomato
Each spice makes a splash
Like a paddle-wheel's thrash
Your Sunday's no longer legato.

Ingredients

- 6 parts vodka
- 1 part sherry
- 2 parts lemon juice
- 12 parts tomato juice
- Salt & pepper, and half a tsp celery salt
- Worcestershire sauce & Tabasco
- 1 large clove garlic
- Celery cut into 3-4 batons
- Large goblets or tumblers

Method
(for mixing a litre)

1. Half crush the garlic clove and push into the tomato juice bottle or carton. Ideally do this the night before
2. Mix the tomato juice with the other ingredients in a large jug
3. Add a dozen shakes of Worcestershire sauce and Tabasco
4. Serve over ice garnished with a slice of lemon and a celery baton
5. For a Virgin Mary leave out the vodka and sherry. It still has a kick and is still delicious!
6. Repeat as necessary but don't get thrashed

Mississippi Oldtimer Dampfschiff

Red Snapper

*R*ed Snapper is even more of a cheat – on two counts! First, it's a variation on a *Proud/Bloody Mary* and secondly, it wasn't invented by me but by a friend James, who as well as being an intrepid sailor in his 1911 yawl, is also a bit of a mixologist. Aboard his vessel one evening we had given him a bottle of *Virgin Proud Mary*. He sailed away with the bottle and spent the next fortnight experimenting. James came up with two breakthrough innovations. He tried gin instead of vodka and he introduced the concept of *Solera*, the Spanish term for gradually topping up the mixture (fractional blending is Wiki's description) resulting in a mixture of ages that slowly grows over time.

James then told me that *Red Snapper* wasn't his invention but that of the Colonsay Hotel on the picturesque island of Colonsay on the West Coast of Scotland. I later found it in *Difford's Guide*, the astonishing book that lists every cocktail known to man, so a *Red Snapper* is not even original to Colonsay. However, the application of *Solera* is novel.

My contribution is to offer Portuguese madeira instead of Spanish sherry – more mellow perhaps, with echoes of Flanders & Swann, and it helps with cultural balance. What to name this multi-aged gin-based *Mary*? I toyed with *Virginny Mary* but it's hard to get rhyme and scan with such an ugly phrase. In any case, *Red Snapper*, with its image of short, sharp, needle-like teeth is perfect. Yes! That's the name for a drink with bite.

Red Snapper

There is something about a Red Snapper
Razored teeth like the front of a gale
A bite like a song by Frank Zappa
Best to grab this cock fish by the tail

There is something about a Red Snapper
With its sinuous base from solera
To balance the gin
And cleanse Spanish sin
Ditch the sherry, instead try madeira.

Ingredients

- 6 parts gin
- 1 part madeira
- 2 parts lemon juice
- 12 parts tomato juice
- Salt & pepper, and half a tsp celery salt
- Worcestershire sauce and Tabasco
- 1 large clove garlic
- Celery cut into 3-4 batons
- Large goblets or tumblers

Method

1. Follow the recipe for a *Proud Mary*
2. For a *Virgin Mary* leave out the gin and madeira.
3. Mix quickly = make it snappy!
4. Repeat as necessary till red-faced like a Snapper

The Red Snapper's razored teeth

Ryde
on the
Storm

There was an old lady from Ryde
Who ate some green apples and died
The apples fermented inside the lamented
And made cider inside her inside

Anonymous

The poor old lady – if only she'd added gin.

These Ryders aren't your typical Hertz van Rental drive-yourself types. They're the real thing – think The Doors at full volume, maybe the Four Horsemen of the Apocalypse (threatening pestilence amongst other nasties), or the Beatles' Apple Bonkers on horseback. A stormy mix of gin, apple cider, lime and ginger beer.

The name is an echo from The Doors' song, spelt "riders". Intriguingly their producer is rumoured to have walked out of the recording studio because he thought the song was 'cocktail music'!

Ryders on the Storm

There is something about the Storm Ryders
Knights gallop with forbidden fruit
The deal has appeal, they're inciders
Drink quickly, the law's in pursuit

There is something about the Storm Ryders
A flavour that's gold 'n delicious
"To avoid the lamented -
Add gin? You're demented!"
The blossomed result is seditious.

Ingredients

The Four Horseman of the Apocalypse. Not a cheery lot but at least one has a glass in his hand

- 2 parts gin
- 1 part apple cider
- 1 part lime juice
- 1 part ginger beer
- Apple slice
- Large goblets or tumblers

Method

1. Mix all ingredients except the ginger beer
2. Pour over crushed ice
3. Add the ginger beer
4. Garnish with apple slices and a cinnamon stick
5. Repeat as necessary, especially when storm-bound

Shopaholic

I was walking with my nightingale through London's Berkeley Square one evening and decided to pop into the Lansdowne Club, a fine building with delightful facilities and excellent food and drink. We resolved to have a cocktail. I forget the name but it was so delicious I asked the barman how to make it.

I have therefore stolen this recipe from the Lansdowne but in recognition that it's really theirs I have named it *Shopaholic*, as a nod towards Harry Gordon Selfridge, the founder of Selfridges & Co. The Lansdowne's building used to be his London house.

It's a bit like a *Negroni* with its bitter sweetness but quite a bit more interesting and the difference in viscosity between the gin/vermouth/Cointreau mix and the Campari creates a beautiful pattern. But do take care to feed the Campari slowly into the bottom of the glass by using a funnel.

You might wonder about "hypergolic". To save you the trouble of looking it up, here's what it means: "(of a rocket propellant) igniting spontaneously on mixing with another substance." Sounds pretty good in a cocktail!

Shopaholic

There is something about Shopaholic
A therapy rooted in retail
The mixture is soon hypergolic
Don't focus too much on the detail

There is something about Shopaholic
A combustible glass full of shopping
With swirly Campari
It's a drinker's safari
The taste is delicious and whopping.

Ingredients

- 4 parts gin
- 1 part dry vermouth
- 1 part Cointreau
- About ½ part Campari
- Cocktail glasses

Selfridge's Oxford Street store

Method

1. Mix the gin, vermouth and Cointreau in a cocktail shaker and cool
2. Pour into glasses
3. Delicately feed in enough Campari to add colour
4. Maybe an olive
5. Repeat therapy as necessary

A Drink With Something In It

(Complete poem)

There is something about a Martini,
A tingle remarkably pleasant;
A yellow, a mellow Martini;
I wish I had one at present.
There is something about a Martini,
Ere the dining and dancing begin,
And to tell you the truth,
It is not the vermouth —
I think that perhaps it's the gin.

There is something about an old-fashioned
That kindles a cardiac glow;
It is soothing and soft and impassioned
As a lyric by Swinburne or Poe.
There is something about an old-fashioned
When dusk has enveloped the sky,
And it may be the ice,
Or the pineapple slice,
But I strongly suspect it's the rye.

There is something about a mint julep.
It is nectar imbibed in a dream,
As fresh as the bud of the tulip,
As cool as the bed of the stream.
There is something about a mint julep,
A fragrance beloved by the lucky.
And perhaps it's the tint
Of the frost and the mint,
But I think it was born in Kentucky.

There is something they put in a highball
That awakens the torpidest brain,
That kindles a spark in the eyeball,
Gliding singing through vein after vein.
There is something they put in a highball
Which you'll notice one day, if you watch;
And it may be the soda,
But judged by the odor,
I rather believe it's the Scotch.

Then here's to the heartening wassail,
Wherever good fellows are found;
Be its master instead of its vassal,
And order the glasses around.
For there's something they put in the wassail
That prevents it from tasting like wicker;
Since it's not tapioca,
Or mustard, or mocha,
I'm forced to conclude it's the liquor.

Ogden Nash (1902-1971)

Ingredients

Spirits

Y ou don't need to splash out on the fanciest gin or rum in the shop but do make sure it packs a decent punch so avoid the 37.5% neutered variety. My regular gin is Tanqueray 43.0%, but I recently bought a bottle of 57% "Naval Strength". Lethal.

And try substituting brandy for rum etc. Perhaps even grappa. That will give your cocktails impact. Just think of Dylan Thomas' graphic description of grappa: 'tastes like an axe'.

Liqueurs

This is where you can have a lot of fun. The recipes in this book are merely suggestions. Try substituting other things. The crèmes are fertile ground – I've suggested fraise and framboise but don't overlook cacao, cassis, menthe or violette. Steer clear of crème de la mer as that's a moisturiser which would add a bit too much viscosity.

After a while you'll differentiate the liqueurs into sweet, bitter, fruity… and other, and you'll develop a feel for what you can and cannot swap.

It's well worth taking a trip to Gerry's, the mixologist's holy grail in Old Compton Street in London's Soho. Gerry's stocks everything known to cocktail-making man. Another fine source is Wynand Fockink in Amsterdam, and any excuse to visit Amsterdam has to be a good one. I inherited a host of fusty bottles from my grandfather (he of port and brandy fame) including a bottle of maraschino that came from Wynand Fockink (remember it's Dutch so the "w" is like "v"). Great as an after-dinner chat-up line: "How's about some Wynand Fockink?"

The other alternative is to make your own. Many people make sloe gin. You can also make "gin" by flavouring vodka. Get some basic supermarket vodka and add botanicals such as basil, cardamon, coriander, cucumber, lemon, seaweed (for gin de la mer) and of course juniper.

Fruit juice

Ideally one always has fresh fruit available, however there may be occasions, like on a sailing boat on the West Coast of Scotland, where this is not possible. So, I keep bottles of pre-squeezed lemon and lime juice and use supermarket juices when I have to. The result is better than you might expect.

Honey water

Put equal parts of runny honey and boiling water in a jug, mix thoroughly then chill. The result is much easier to dissolve in a cocktail than sugar.

Grenadine

A useful non-alcoholic sweetener, made from pomegranate seeds. But use cautiously as it is very sweet.

Raspberry syrup

Bring 200g raspberries, 50g sugar and 300ml water to boil, simmer for 10 minutes, strain off the biggest bits and sieve.

Rhubarb syrup

Bring c. 375g rhubarb, 50g sugar, 1 tbsp water to boil then turn the heat off. Once cooled drain off the juice. The remaining fruit will then need a bit more cooking before it's nice to eat, this just being a by-product of the core cocktail process.

Garnish

Garnish is part of the visual fun that goes with cocktails. Here are a few ideas:

- *Cherries* – maraschino cherries from Luxardo, makers of the exquisite maraschino liqueur are delicious (try them with ice cream!) but use sparingly in drinks as they are strongly flavoured and can take charge. You may be better off with Opies Cocktail Cherries

- *Citrus fruit twists* – grapefruit, lemon, lime, orange. Cut a slice, not too thin (7-8mm), lay it flat, cut through the skin at one point then carefully chop out the fruit. Then give it a neat little twist and position on the edge of a glass

- *Frozen fruit slices* – a variation on *Twists*. Slice medium thick (5mm) then cut in half and put in a box in the freezer. Use them for combined garnish plus cooling

- *Herbs* – for example, basil in an *Asian Flew*, mint – always a good choice in e.g. a *Bum's Rush*, a *Flora Dora* or a *Noonday Gun*. Maybe a sprig of coriander here and there

- *Olives* – no introduction needed. Much admired in an *Ogden Nash*

- *Roasted fruit* – cut thin (3-4mm) slices of your fruit (usual suspects), cut them in half, lay them on greaseproof paper in a roasting dish, and roast in the oven at 125°C for at least an hour until they are thoroughly dried out and beginning to turn dark

- *Soft fruit* – Raspberries are good where you're using raspberry syrup. Strawberries are best sliced

Equipment

Cocktail shaker

A decent shaker is essential. The most important feature is that it doesn't leak. Like cream jugs that don't pour, it's surprising how many cocktail shakers do leak. You could be old-fashioned and try it out in a shop before you part with your cash!

There are some fun ones. I have a few – my favourites are one sprouting a pineapple and another with a rabbit's head.

The other choice is to go for a pair of shaking tins. Makes you look like a pro!

Cocktailing rules dictate that mixtures with cloudy ingredients like fruit juice should be shaken whilst those with clear ingredients should be stirred, as shaking the ice achieves better aeration. However, there are plenty of rule-breakers, just think of Bond.

Glasses

I've used old-fashioned British descriptions like goblet or tumbler rather than the American terms like highball. Technically a highball is probably taller than a tumbler, otherwise no difference. In times gone by a tumbler used to have a convex base, hence its name, which meant the drinker had to finish his drink. Dangerous. For short cocktails a classic saucer is beautiful. You can sometimes pick them up in antique shops but there are also some pretty modern imitations, e.g. from www.thevintagelist.co.uk.

Other Useful Bits of Kit

- *Cocktail Sticks*. Handy for garnish like cherries, olives or raspberries. Stainless steel can be smart, silver even better

- *A Funnel*. Saves wasting precious fluid by spraying it everywhere

- A measure, technically known as a *Jigger*, is handy, particularly if you're fairly new to mixing cocktails. After a while you'll wing it (or maybe sling it) with interesting consequences

- A see-through *Measuring Jug*. Useful if you're making large quantities

- A *Sodastream*. This enables you to make just the amount of ginger beer you want – use one of the ginger cordials, Belvoir is the best

- A *Squeezer*, and if you're making *Pampered Goose* (grapefruit) an industrial one is essential. Ours weighs a ton so also handy for tackling burglars

- A *Julep Strainer* can be useful

- A pair of *Tongs*. Good for handling garnish

Hangover Cures

This should really be a guest column. Everyone will have the perfect solution, be it raw eggs, a half marathon, a bunch of bananas or deep inhalation of garden shed chemicals.

Pick Me Up

I was once given a bottle of something called *Pick Me Up*. I'd gone to a stag do on a Thursday and it was quite a heavy night. A meeting on Friday morning called for an intelligent demeanour. Panic!

I reached into the bathroom cabinet hoping for some sort of salvation, like Alka Selzer (with echoes of comedian Shelly Berman saying "Oh God, oh my God, oh Alka Selzer don't fizz..."). My eyes alighted on the small bottle *Pick Me Up*. Magic!

I whipped the top off and took a hefty swig. The result was a full-scale nuclear attack! A ball of fire powered through my body like the fuse on a Brock's rocket, my fingers jittered, my toes almost flew off their joints, my heart went berserk, a good 200 bpm. After about five minutes of sheer hell my body calmed down, with a slightly smug "OK, we handled that, what next?" sort of feel. I looked at the *Pick Me Up* label: "one teaspoonful diluted with five parts water". No wonder my body had gone into full defence mode, I'd had half the bottle neat. Tough, but it cured my hangover!

Pick Me Up came from a chemist dating from 1790 in St James,

London, called D R Harris (now moved to Piccadilly). A few years ago I went in and asked for *Pick Me Up*, as I thought it might be a good present for my son who was then in the army. A puzzled girl said she couldn't help but an older gentleman had overheard and explained that sadly they were no longer allowed to sell it. No doubt it was some mandarin's bright idea.

Guess what?! D R Harris is once again selling *Pick Me Up*. Now marketed as a cocktail bitters, their website **www.drharris.co.uk/ product/the-original-pick-me-up** explains how to morph it into the original 'morning reviver'. As they say "any signs of jadedness will dissipate and all will be right with the world".

Other Cures

These broadly fall into two buckets (and if you have any sense you'll have a bucket to hand after a heavy night): "Medicinal" and Random.

"Medicinal"

When I was growing up medicines used to be evil-tasting. I recall a cough mixture that seemed to be made from rotting vegetables. There was no chance of getting addicted to these: the whole idea was to encourage one to get well pretty damned quickly.

There's a bunch of herbal potions that share some of the cough mixture characteristics. Not so the modern version of *Pick Me Up* – D R Harris say that the original *Pick Me Up* "was favoured far-and-wide for its effectiveness, however, it was not prized for its taste or aroma". Following reformulation it has been relaunched as something that makes your cocktails taste good!

Other herbal candidates include *Fernet Branca*, *Underberg* and *Jägermeister* (the latter two both come from the wonderfully named Kräuterlikörs family). *Fernet Branc*a started out as a cure for cholera and menstrual cramps then took off after a Madonna-like repositioning during American Prohibition. *Underberg* includes "aromatic, digestion-stimulating, relaxing and calming active substances" which sounds like a good start for a hangover cure. Apparently, it contains rhubarb from China (useful for *Barbie Doll*). According to Wiki, *Jägermeister* does **not** contain elk blood! But it is used in some extraordinarily-named cocktails like *The Four Horsemen of the Apocalypse* (cf the reference to this in our *Ryders on the Storm*), and *Red-headed Slut*, as well as the better-known *Jägerbomb*.

Random

Nowadays, medicine is sweet-tasting – think cough mixture Benylin. Benylin was first cousin to Concord(e), whose label described it as "an unusually light and refreshing, slightly sparkling, British wine". I'll never forget it. I shared a bottle en route to the Dundee flea market, where I bought a giant papier-mâché head and a dinner jacket, which I used for over 20 years, for the combined price of £1.50 (it was the early 1970's). British wine was not your classic Camel Valley *premier cru*. It was "made" in Britain from imported grapes and Concord(e) tasted just like Benylin that had done time in a Sodastream.

Benylin is not known as a hangover cure, at least not yet. Room for a pioneer.

Other solutions...

... include:

- isotonic drinks like Lucozade and hydration tablets such as O.R.S (not a French bear, this is the non-U version), or you can make your own – assuming you're fit enough to surf the internet to find a recipe designed for high intensity sportsmen who dehydrate...

- very sweet foods like banana muffins or chocolate fudge cake

- bouillon soup (recommended by the NHS, but beware, bouillon could lead you astray into *Highland Bull* territory)

- lots of carbs, in the shape of a hearty breakfast

- hair of the dog – more alcohol. This is supposed to work because the extra alcohol doesn't get converted into formaldehyde as it normally does. Formaldehyde is the stuff that undertakers use to stiffen up 'stiffs' (at high risk to themselves, I should add) so no wonder stopping your body making it is a good thing!

- the ultimate hair of the dog has to be a *Corpse Reviver*. It comes in a variety of forms, *Corpse Reviver No.1*, *No.2* and *No.2A*. This recipe is for a *No.2*. Equal parts gin, curaçao (usually Cointreau), lemon juice and Lillet Blanc (or Cocchi Americano or Swedish Punsch), plus a few dashes of absinthe. This reminds me of Frank Muir's lovely line about the Impressionists admiring Manet's *Dejeuner sur l'herbe* "they were all there, apart from Van Gogh, conspicuous by his absinthe, ear today gone tomorrow". The Savoy Cocktail Book's description of the *No.2* recipe noted that "Four of these taken in swift succession will un-revive the corpse again." Beware!

- supplements like ginseng, prickly pear, ginger and borage oil (I can't vouch for any of these!)

- *a Prairie Oyster*. This is a raw egg (carefully deshelled so as not to break the yoke), salt & pepper, Worcestershire sauce and Tabasco. People try to prove it scientifically but its claim to success as a hangover cure is more likely to be on the 'rotting vegetable' principle, i.e. it tastes so awful that it just **must** be good for you

Cocktails
&
Kicktails
App

The "Shaker" App is a natural and modern companion to this book. It is available for download from the Rowan Books website **https://rowanbooks.co.uk/cocktails/cocktails-app/** – or scan the QR code below.

The full version contains recipes for all the cocktails in the *Cocktails & Kicktails* book and some 400 others. It is a paid-for App and is free to those who have bought the book off the Rowan Books website.

The App has lots of useful features:

- *Recipes*. Find a *Cocktails & Kicktails* recipe when you don't have the book with you

- *Ingredients*. An interactive version of the "Cocktails at a

Glance" ingredients matrix in the book

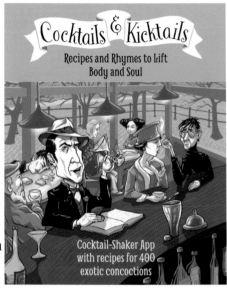

Cocktails & Kicktails

Recipes and Rhymes to Lift Body and Soul

Cocktail-Shaker App with recipes for 400 exotic concoctions

- *Poetry*. Poems about the cocktails and the opportunity to submit a poem for possible future publication

- *Shaker*. What can I make? Enter a few ingredients you have to hand and discover what cocktails you can make with them. Just (cocktail) shake your phone and up pops a recipe. Don't fancy that? Shake it again!

- *Party Planner*. How much do I need? Work out how much of each ingredient you need to make a particular cocktail for a given number of people

- *Sketches*. Background to a cocktail's origins.

Bibliography & Credits

Books to read

There is a rich vein of books about cocktails, most of which contain recipes. Jerry Thomas probably kicked off the trend with *The Bartender's Guide* in 1862, followed by Harry Johnson 20 years later with *The Bartender's Manual* (mixologists were getting more hands-on by now). And then in the 1930's after prohibition was lifted authors really got into gear: Harry Craddock wrote *The Savoy Cocktail Book* in 1930, containing some 750 recipes, the *Café Royal Cocktail Book* came out in 1937, and *The Gentleman's Companion* by Charles H Baker Junior in 1939, dispelling the notion that cocktails were for arrivistes. Post the Second World War, David Embury's *The Fine Art of Mixing Drinks* was published in 1949, the same year that Esquire Magazine started its *Handbook for Hosts*. An excellent history of cocktails is *Vintage Spirits and Forgotten Cocktails* by Ted Haigh's (aka Dr Cocktail); it also contains some delicious long-lost recipes.

Today there are myriads of cocktail recipe books and online sites. *Difford's Guide* by Simon Difford is an amazing volume with recipes, histoires and first-class photographs for over 1,500 cocktails. Maybe some of those in *Cocktails & Kicktails* will one day make it in to *Difford's* – that would be the ultimate accolade. There are also themed cocktail books, tying cocktails to art,

66

music or literature. One of the best is *Tequila Mockingbird* by Tim Federle – the title says it all!

Credits and Permissions

All illustrations by Gareth Southwell; all photographs of cocktails by Michael Brooks; other photographs by the author, except as stated: frontispiece, "London policeman testing lifejackets", Museum of London; vi, "George VI and Queen Elizabeth wearing Mae West lifejackets", Flickr; 8, "Fiat's Lingotto test track", Adobe Stock; "Fiat 124 Sport Coupé", by GIELDAklasykow; 10, "Barbie Doll", Adobe Stock; 12, "East Berlin Cold War era apartments", Adobe Stock; "Silvio Berlusconi" by Brengola-Diena and Wenn; 14, "Red Hot Chilli Piper" and "Strip the Willow" by Wendy Stewart; 18, "The Author and his Wife dance a Foredeck Reel" by Miranda Delmar-Morgan; 20, "Hartley's New Jam", Adobe Stock; "Pyjama Party anyone?", Flickr; 24, "Horny Highland Bull with heather and moss", Adobe Stock; 26, "Mexican Coat of Arms", Wikimedia Commons; 28, "Lagonda in ford", Motoring Picture Library; 30, "The Porters Stone" by Kim Traynor, Wikimedia Commons; 32, "Margarita (actually Mae West)", Getty Images; 34, "Judge's gavel", Adobe Stock; 36, "The Noonday Gun", Adobe Stock; 38, "Ogden Nash", Getty Images; 40, "Howard Hughes' Spruce Goose" by Eric Gardner, Flickr; 42, images in "A peacock morphs into a flamingo", Adobe Stock; 44, "Mississippi Oldtimer Dampfschiff", Adobe Stock; 46, "The Red Snapper's razored teeth", Adobe Stock; 48, "The Four Horsemen of the Apocalypse", Adobe Stock; 50, "Selfridge's Oxford Street store", copyright Business Matters magazine; 55-56, garnish images, Adobe Stock; 59, "Pick-Me-Up", D.R.Harris & Co. Ltd. Reproduction rights as follows: 51, "A drink with something in it" and extract (iv) from *Candy is Dandy* by Ogden Nash (Edition 1994, André Deutsch) by kind permission of Welbeck Publishing Limited; 29, Extract from "The Berry fields o Blair" by Belle Stewart.

Acknowledgements

Many moons ago when I was in my early 20's I stayed with a girlfriend's parents. Her lovely father asked me after dinner what I collected. I didn't collect anything and worried how to reply. Then came the inspiration: "Anecdotes".

One of the thank yous in this book is to my many friends and relations who have provided anecdotes, often through their own actions as much as storytelling, and much other background to the thinking behind this book. They have all been subjected over the years to my experiments and almost without exception they're a robust lot – they keep coming back for more. Some of them are named in the book, others have contributed hugely but there isn't room to mention everyone. Anyway, thank you.

Many of you have been kind enough to edit, proof read, improve rhymes, and generally offer constructive criticism. This has helped beyond measure.

Michael Brooks and Annemarie Gibson of Circmedia have taken the superb photographs (please do give them back!). Clive Woodman and Angela Lilienthal of Live Icom have built the super-nifty App with its brilliant cocktail shaker feature, the invention of my son-in-law Henry. Gareth Southwell has drawn some lovely images, including the cover pages and turned my rough and ready graphics into beautiful reality.

My brother-in-law Keith Morris, a partner in Rowan Books, has been a tower of strength. He has the rare combination of a career in document management with a love for books and poetry and has provided consistent, patient and intelligent advice.

Finally, to my immediate family. Particularly to my Darling Bond-Girl wife Wendy, who along with every ounce of advice and support along the way has supplied what must be one of the best review comments for any author. And to our six children and their lovely spouses, partners and now offspring. You have all offered criticism, love and support.

Thank you.

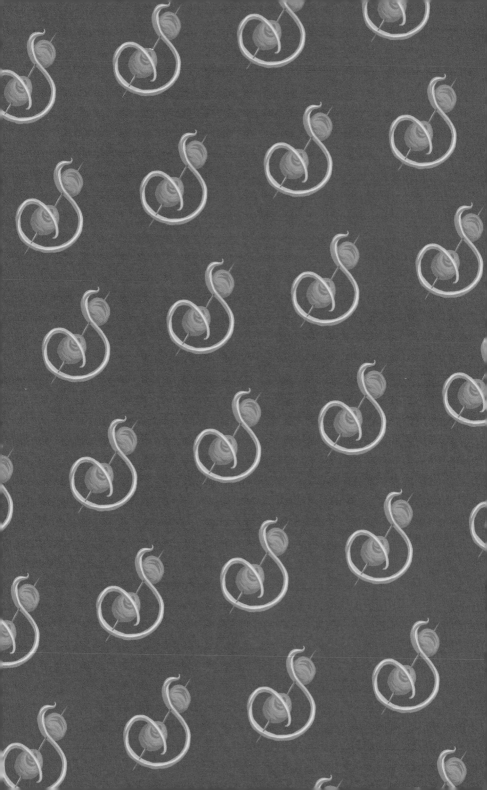